Introduction

What Is Iron and Why Do I Need It?

Iron Deficiency Anemia: What It Is and How to Cope With and Prevent It

All You Need to Know About Iron Supplements

Foods That Support the Absorption of Iron

Iron-Rich Foods

Lifestyle Changes That Can Improve Iron Intake

Vegans, Vegetarians, and Iron Deficiency

Hemochromatosis

Low-Iron Recipe Ideas for Sufferers of Hemochromatosis

Iron-Rich Recipes for Vegans and Vegetarians

Iron-Rich Recipes and Tips for Meat-Eaters

10 Steps Ahead

Introduction

There is an unfortunate need for a book on a diet for those who are lacking iron. Anemia is a common problem and can plague many types of people. When we are lacking in iron, it can sometimes seem like life is just too hard. We are tired and bruise and hurt easily. Not only that, but it can be difficult to concentrate and remember the things that we are told and tasks that need to be accomplished.

All of these consequences of living without enough iron in the bloodstream can lead to serious health issues, so it is more important than ever to begin to take action.

If you have already been diagnosed with anemia, you have been living with low iron for too long. If you are embarking on a lifestyle change such as veganism or vegetarianism, or you simply have cut out sources of iron from your diet for personal reasons, supplementing iron is a big step in order to remain healthy.

But why can't we just pop an iron pill and move on?

Unfortunately, studies have shown that supplements are not always adequate ways for our bodies to receive nutrients. Not only that, but taking iron supplements won't guarantee that our bodies even absorb the iron that we take.

With that in mind, we are going to embark upon a journey to discover exactly what it means for our bodies to live without iron in our diets and what we can do to ensure that we are receiving adequate nutrition.

At the end of the book, a few recipes will be offered for those who are new to a life with low iron in their diets, along with suggestions for people who have been living with anemia for a long time. It's time to begin to do something about all of this and this book will show you how.

WHAT IS IRON AND WHY DO I NEED IT?

Most of us understand that having heavy metals in the body can be a very bad thing. For example, studies have proven that an accumulation of heavy metals in the bloodstream, such as aluminum, are linked with neurological disorders, including, but not limited to, Alzheimer's disease and dementia. So why is it so important to make sure that we are getting enough of the heavy metal iron in our bodies?

The reality is that iron is necessary for almost all living things to function. Everybody, from humans to elephants to bacteria, has some reliance on iron. Iron is a bio-element that helps electrons move throughout the body, and more or less plays a role in where electrons go and what they do.

Iron: Ferrous State and Ferric State

There are two different states of iron. The first is the ferrous state. In a ferrous state, iron donates electrons and offers them up to where they need to be. In the other, the ferric state, iron accepts electrons from other places. Whether iron is acting as an electron donor or an acceptor, it plays a crucial role in mediating the reactions of enzymes by either oxidizing them, turning them into rust, or reducing the enzymes.

Our bodies don't necessarily rust, but they do have a reliance on this bio-element. The body needs iron to help move oxygen throughout the body and to animate cells with energy. This process is known as cellular respiration.

Recommended Daily Iron Intake

Wow, you may think, maybe I should go out and eat nothing but iron!

That would be a mistake. Iron is as useful as it is dangerous. To avoid toxicity, it is recommended to get only the daily amount of iron recommended by nutritionists. Iron intake is variable depending on your age and sex.

Currently, the recommended value of iron intake is as follows:

- Females seven to 12 months old – 11mg

- Males seven to 12 months old – 11mg

- Females one to three years old – 7mg

- Males one to three years old – 7 mg

- Females four to eight years old – 10mg

- Males four to eight years old – 10 mg

- Females nine to 13 years old – 8 mg

- Males nine to 13 years old – 8 mg

- Females 14-18 years old – 15mg

- Males 14-18 years old – 11mg

- Females 19-50 years old – 18mg

- Males 19-50 years old – 8mg

- Females 51 years and older – 8mg

- Males 51 years and older – 8mg

Women who are pregnant require 27mg of iron intake and if lactating, should have 10 mg if they are between 14-18 years old, or 9mg if they are 19-50 years old.

Iron and Hemoglobin

The most important function of iron in a human body is to bring oxygen into the body's tissues. It works to carry air from the lungs to the muscles and tendons using the ferrous and ferric states briefly discussed in the former chapter. Without iron in the hemoglobin, the component that makes this transfer possible in the body, then we start to see some problems.

Hemoglobin is an element associated with the blood because it is found in red blood cells. Oxygen is carried through the body in these blood cells through the hemoglobin from the lungs. As it gives oxygen to the body's muscles and tissues, it exchanges the oxygen for carbon dioxide. When it returns back to the lungs, it brings that carbon dioxide back with it and deposits it in the lungs as well.

Most of us are probably familiar with the fact that we breathe in oxygen and bring out carbon dioxide. That process is an essential cycle for the body and it happens on a microscopic as well as macroscopic scale in this case. The oxygen we breathe in is transported from the lungs on the hemoglobin. The hemoglobin carries it through the body's bloodstream and deposits it where it needs to be in order to function the best. When it deposits the oxygen in the tissues, it is exchanged with carbon dioxide. The carbon dioxide is then expelled out of the body from the lungs.

It is a constant process that allows our bodies to be as healthy as they possibly can be. Without it, we enter into dangerous territory.

What Is Hemoglobin?

Hemoglobin is formed from four protein molecules that make up a chain. In the chain are alpha-globulin and beta-globulin. Generally, beta-globulin chains are only formed as we grow and are rarely seen in babies and young children.

Hemoglobin is so named because of the compound heme. This is where the iron atom is located within the chain so that we can move oxygen throughout our body. Without hemoglobin, our blood cells would not have the uniform shape of a healthy blood cell, so it is possible for blood cells to become disfigured and run into mobility issues.

Generally, we want to see a specific range of hemoglobin in the blood cells and if that range goes too high or too low, then there are problems. Generally, the problem is too little iron being absorbed by the body and impeding the development of hemoglobin. As with most measurements, age and sex play a role in determining the preferred amount of hemoglobin that should be found in the body.

It isn't an exact number because all laboratories may have different standards of measurement, so results may vary. But these are the most approximate amounts of hemoglobin that should be present in the body at any given time. If these numbers are too low or too high, issues can arise.

Pregnant women should be especially careful in this case because too much hemoglobin could result in stillbirths, while not enough hemoglobin might cause babies to be born prematurely or underweight. Because of this, pregnant women should make sure that they are keeping hemoglobin levels even: not too high, nor too low.

The range of hemoglobin preferred is as follows:

•Infants (male and female) under a week of age: 17-22gm per hundred milliliters

•Infants (male and female) one week old: 15-20gm per hundred milliliters

•Infants (male and female) one month old: 11-15gm per hundred milliliters

•Children (male and female) one month old through 18 years old: 11-13gm per hundred milliliters

•Adult males 18-40 years of age: 14-18gm per hundred milliliters

•Adult females 18-40 years of age: 12-15gm per hundred milliliters

•Males beyond middle age: 12.4-14.9gm per hundred milliliters

•Females beyond middle age: 11.7gm-13.8gm per hundred milliliters

Overall, it can be important to have the proper levels of hemoglobin. If you fall above or below the standard levels of hemoglobin in the body, that means that you are lacking in iron or getting too much iron, and may end up having health problems as a result.

What Happens When Red Blood Cells Lack Hemoglobin?

Our bodies will generally produce red blood cells, but whether these blood cells contain hemoglobin or not is really a question of how much iron we are getting in the body. When we aren't receiving the right amount of iron, the protein compound known as hemoglobin will become a lot scarcer. This means that our bodies are going to have some issues.

As mentioned previously, without hemoglobin, our tissues and muscles would not receive the oxygen necessary in ensuring our good health. Once our stores of iron have been sufficiently depleted, our bodies will also begin to produce fewer red blood cells. This can be an issue. Not only that, but when the body is able to produce red blood cells, these cells will be lacking in the necessary compound hemoglobin.

To summarize, once our body has been depleted of our iron stores and begins to produce fewer blood cells, and those blood cells are lacking in the hemoglobin necessary in keeping our bodies healthy and functioning, a specific issue can arise known as anemia. Anemia can have many different causes, iron deficiency being one of the most common. This affliction will be discussed in a later chapter.

Iron Deficiency and Excess Iron In the Body

Iron deficiency can be a very dangerous affliction. But what most people don't realize is that low iron in the body isn't just a problem physically. It can be an issue psychologically as well.

Unfortunately, suffering from low iron is associated with complications that range anywhere from paranoia to anemia. Because iron is so important to our physical and mental health, it is important to make sure that we are getting enough iron in our diet.

However, there is also such a thing as receiving too much iron in the body. Too much of a good thing isn't always necessarily the answer. In fact, excess iron in the body can also cause issues. Because it is a heavy metal, we have to be careful to make sure we maintain proper iron levels or face serious consequences.

Heme and Non-Heme Iron

The iron we receive from our diet comes in two forms. These include heme iron and non-heme iron. The differences in these two types of iron are the sources from which they are derived. Heme iron is received from animal sources, such as seafood, red meat, and poultry. Non-heme iron comes from plants and foods that are fortified with iron.

While heme iron is generally believed to be easier for the body to absorb and utilize, it is also considered a little bit more dangerous. Health effects of heme iron include increased risk of issues such as heart disease, stroke, and cancer. It may also negatively impact the metabolic system.

Sometimes, too much meat consumption can negatively impact the body, and even lead to complications later in life associated with an overload of iron in the body. It is important to eat a nutrient-rich and diverse diet to avoid complications with heme and non-heme iron in the body.

How Does Iron Deficiency Happen?

Unfortunately, iron deficiency is one of the most common vitamin and mineral deficiencies known to North America. It is a very easy thing to miss, and its importance is rarely stressed when nutrition is discussed. However, having a lack of hemoglobin in the body can be very dangerous to our mental and physical functioning.

Sometimes, we might develop an iron deficiency because we have a unique hemoglobin structure. When our hemoglobin structures are abnormal, this can lead to a deficiency of iron in our blood. For example, people with thalassemia and sickle cell anemia may find that they are prone to iron deficiencies.

Another way iron deficiencies might develop is if we are in unfortunate accidents or have health issues that lead to a large quantity of blood lost. We may lose blood from a car accident, kidney failure, or any other type of traumatic injury. Sometimes, it isn't an accident at all, and the reason we have lost a lot of blood is because we have chosen to donate blood on a regular basis. Whatever the reason, large quantities of blood loss can be a significant cause of iron deficiency anemia.

Women who are pregnant and young women with heavy periods are also at high risk. Pregnant women, in particular, are vulnerable as their bodies go through a series of physical changes, including assigning blood to the uterus, where they use it to support the growth of the babies inside of them. But as mentioned previously, that makes it all the more important to have hemoglobin levels as close to normal as possible.

Sometimes, we simply have a difficult time absorbing iron, no matter how much we eat. When this is the case, it is often due to health problems or gastrointestinal surgeries. For example, people with celiac disease often have only a restricted amount of iron that the body is able to absorb at one time.

Cancer can also be a cause of iron deficiency. When red blood cell synthesis is suppressed by drugs that are a part of chemotherapy treatments or bone marrow is replaced by cancerous cells, these can both deplete iron in the system. It's an unfortunate result of an already heart-wrenching disease.

Another issue that can lead to iron deficiency anemia is internal bleeding. It sounds very scary, and indeed can be. Things like ulcers and polyps are common causes of internal bleeding. Anemia can also occur if over-the-counter pain medications like aspirin are frequently used. Unfortunately, while they promise to help us feel better, a common side effect of using these "medications" is bleeding in the stomach. Uterine fibroids have also been diagnosed as a cause of iron deficiency anemia. When these fibroids develop, they can cause intense pain in the abdomen and a heavy menstrual flow, which has also been linked to anemia.

Finally, and possibly most commonly, an inadequate diet can be the result of iron deficiency. If the body doesn't receive enough vitamin B12, folate, or iron, it can make it very difficult for iron to remain in the body or be absorbed and utilized for its proper function.

Symptoms of Iron Deficiency

Sometimes we don't realize there is a problem until it is too late. However, if we are diligent, it is possible to catch warning signs of iron deficiency before they turn too serious. Regardless, iron deficiency is an affliction that can be treated with relative ease by incorporating lifestyle changes that make it easier for our bodies to receive and absorb iron. Here are some symptoms of iron deficiency to look out for.

- Lethargy
- Fatigue
- Less effective immune system functioning
- Inflammation of the tongue
- Fluctuations in body temperature
- Fragile finger and toe nails
- Decreased performance, whether at school or work
- Slow brain development
- Pale skin
- Strange cravings, such as the desire to eat dirt
- Irregular heartbeat
- Shortness of breath
- Strange creeping feelings in the legs
- Swelling of the tongue
- Sore tongue
- Difficulty in warming extremities, such as hands and feet

- Decreased cognitive functioning
- Difficulties in doing physical work
- Memory loss and decreased function of the memory
- Decreased mental functions

As you can tell, these can be serious issues that should be tended to at once. This is especially true if pregnant. Mothers with iron deficiencies have a greater chance of giving birth to small babies with lower life expectancies.

Symptoms of Excess Iron

Getting too much iron is usually not an issue that most people talk often about. Usually, anemia is the star of the show when it comes to conversations about iron. However, it is possible for excess iron to build up in the system, and once a person reaches the age of 40 and above, complications from built up iron in the system may surface.

Symptoms of excess iron, although subtle, may be noted early. These symptoms include:

- Incontinence or frequent urination
- Joint pain
- Fatigue
- Lethargy
- Tiredness
- Weight loss
- Difficulty performing physical work

If symptoms of excess iron are caught early, you may be diagnosed with excess iron in the blood, a condition known as hemochromatosis. Hemochromatosis will be discussed further in a later section.

Iron Deficiency and Mental Health

Sometimes we may have an iron deficiency and don't even know it. This can cause mental responses to our deficiency that may otherwise be attributed to external factors and irritants when in reality, it is a lack of iron that is contributing to these health problems.

Mental and emotional complications of low iron in the body are often overlooked. However, iron deficiency can often contribute to depression, anxiety, and other difficulties in mental functioning. If you are not receiving enough iron, or your body isn't absorbing iron properly, you may be at risk.

The following are some of the mental and emotional complications that can be associated with an iron deficiency:

- Depression
- Anxiety
- Irritability
- Extreme fatigue
- Appetite loss
- Panic attacks
- Insomnia
- Chest tightness
- Irregular heartbeat
- Mood swings
- Helplessness
- Sadness
- Irregular heart rhythms
- Visual disturbances
- Headaches

- Feelings of dread
- Preoccupation with death or dying
- Muscle weakness
- Issues swallowing/choking
- Restless leg syndrome
- Feelings of unsteadiness/vertigo
- Dizziness
- Motion sickness
- Inability to focus
- Difficulty reading and concentrating
- Difficulty completing simple tasks
- Stress

Overall, the mental toll that an iron deficiency can have on the body is extreme. It can be very frustrating to live with the physical and mental symptoms of an iron deficiency. If you suspect you have low iron, visit a doctor as soon as possible, or continue reading on to find ways to remedy this affliction and begin to turn your life around to get back on track as soon as possible.

IRON DEFICIENCY ANEMIA: WHAT IT IS AND HOW TO COPE WITH AND PREVENT IT

Iron deficiency anemia is the specific title for people whose bodies are lacking in red blood cells and hemoglobin because of an iron deficiency. This particular ailment is the most common anemia issue and can sometimes be brought on by decisions that we make on a daily basis. Little things, like the choices we make in our diet, can play a big role when it comes to our health, and we often don't realize just how much power we have over how we feel.

Sometimes the cause of iron deficiency anemia can be simple, such as heavy blood loss during a woman's menstrual cycle. Women who experience blood loss during pregnancy may also develop this specific type of anemia.

For the most part, iron deficiency anemia is not a life-threatening condition. Despite that, there are many forms of anemia that require special attention. Regardless of the fact that a slight iron deficiency is not considered harmful, many people don't realize that they are suffering from this condition and when left untreated it can become dangerous. Because of the important function of iron, if hemoglobin is decreased in the red blood cells, it means that the heart has to work harder in order to distribute oxygen throughout the body.

Unfortunately, this can lead to an irregular heartbeat in some cases or an enlarged heart in others. Both of these pose a serious health risk and if left untreated, they can even cause heart failure to occur. This is when an iron deficiency goes from being inconvenient to being lethal.

How to Prevent Iron Deficiency Anemia

It is possible that if you are reading this book, you are already suffering from iron deficiency anemia. Whether or not you have already been diagnosed with anemia or you are simply worried about living a lifestyle that is low in iron, there are ways that you can make sure to prevent iron deficiency anemia from happening to you, or getting worse if it already has happened.

The first way to prevent iron deficiency anemia seems fairly intuitive. Simply eat more iron. There is a chapter in this book entirely dedicated to iron-rich foods. Try incorporating these foods into your diet on a daily basis and you will be closer to preventing anemia from happening to you or worsening.

The second way to prevent iron deficiency anemia is to eat foods that support the absorption of iron. Whether we are eating enough iron or not, there are other factors at play when it comes to the absorption of iron in our bodies. If our bodies aren't capable of absorbing enough iron, that comes down to the foods that we are eating and the other nutrients we may be deficient in, such as B12 and folates. This is especially common in vegan and vegetarian diets. Learning more about foods that support iron absorption in the body is key, and a whole chapter will be dedicated to these foods as well.

The third way to ensure that iron deficiency anemia passes you by is to combine consuming iron with eating vitamin C. Vitamin C is one of the many nutrients that our bodies need a healthy supply of, and this is very evident when it comes to the absorption of iron. Eating iron-rich foods, such as spinach, with vitamin C-rich foods, such as oranges, is a great way to make sure that our bodies are ready to absorb the iron that we give it.

What to Do When Diagnosed With Iron Deficiency Anemia

Living with any kind of medical problem can be very difficult, especially when these issues require changes to be made to our daily routines and diets. Unfortunately, that is always going to be the case when our bodies are lacking in vitamins and nutrients. Without these nutrients, our bodies will gradually grow weaker and complications may arise.

When you are officially diagnosed with iron deficiency anemia, it is important to get a good idea of the scope of the problem. If you have been living on a diet that is severely lacking in iron for several years, complications may arise from that, and these complications should be dealt with through medical attention. Do not attempt to self-treat iron deficiency anemia, as we are all different and our bodies require specific vitamins and minerals to function properly.

If you are diagnosed with iron deficiency anemia, there are a few steps that you should take immediately. The first is to speak with your doctor about appropriate supplements, not only for iron but for vitamin B12 and folates as well, as these deficiencies are often found alongside the iron deficiency and come hand-in-hand. Once you have discussed the proper supplementation that is right for you, then you are going to be responsible for improving your diet and making sure that you are getting enough vitamins and minerals to maintain a healthy lifestyle.

It is very important that you learn as much about the specific type of anemia that you have. Be open and honest with your doctors, as they will often withhold treatment until they have pinpointed the underlying cause of your ailment. When they have a good idea of what is causing your issues, only then will they feel comfortable deciding upon a line of action to help you to treat your iron deficiency.

When to Consult a Doctor

Unfortunately, anemia that can be fixed and prevented purely through the diet is not the only type of anemia that can develop. While the suggestions mentioned above are great ways to help iron enter the body, there are some times when medical intervention is required to treat your specific type of anemia.

While diet is a crucial factor in living with anemia, there are times when your specific medical needs will not be fixed by diet alone. For example, those with celiac disease or other gastrointestinal diseases will need the help of a doctor to get proper nutrition.

Other types of anemia that should be dealt with by an experienced medical care practitioner who is well-educated on your specific case include Crohn's disease, aplastic anemia, cancer-induced anemia, and hemolytic anemia. All of these forms of anemia require medical attention and the information in this book should not be used as a substitute for responsible medical advice.

Coping With Iron Deficiency Anemia

Depending on how far along it is, the typical understanding is that anemia is something that can be easily treated. However, complications from long-term anemia can be a little bit more dangerous, such as heart growth or irregular heartbeats.

Fortunately, most people catch anemia early on, and coping with it can be easy. Most of the time, supplements will be involved, and their necessity may last anywhere from a few months to a year or more, depending on what your doctor recommends. It is important to follow instructions and pay close attention to any symptoms that the iron supplements you are taking cause you to have, as it can become dangerous to put too much iron in the body.

When you are taking supplements, make sure to regularly consult with your doctor and ask to change the supplements if you find yourself suffering from gastrointestinal distress or other side effects from the supplements. While you are taking the supplements, try to get into the habit of eating iron-rich foods and foods that will support the absorption of iron in your system.

Listen carefully to any orders and recommendations given to you by your doctor and follow them until you are in the clear. In some cases, you may end up needing to receive blood or an IV to help deal with severe iron deficiency. Iron deficiency anemia isn't always a serious problem, but when it persists for too long, complications may become severe. Do whatever is necessary to overcome these obstacles and balance out your deficiency once and for all.

ALL YOU NEED TO KNOW ABOUT IRON SUPPLEMENTS

The unfortunate fact of the matter is that with any diet that is low in anything, supplements are going to be the best way to receive more nutrition. It is almost guaranteed that if you are struggling with iron deficiency anemia, you will be prescribed an iron supplement to help you to cope with this inadequacy in your diet. However, there are many questions and concerns that you might have when it comes to taking a supplement to improve your health. This chapter will go through the most common questions associated with iron supplements.

Ferrous Versus Ferric Iron

It is hard to tell which type of iron supplement you should be taking without medical intervention. There are two main types of iron supplements available and while each have their own benefits, it is important to consult a doctor before attempting to treat iron deficiency anemia with supplements.

The majority of iron supplements are made of ferrous iron, simply because it is a little bit easier on the body and can be absorbed better. There are three subcategories of ferrous iron. Ferrous fumarate, ferrous sulfate, and ferrous gluconate are most often prescribed to those who are suffering from an iron deficiency. This is because they are generally the fastest way to introduce iron into a body that is suffering from iron deficiency.

Unfortunately for our bodies, ferric iron is less often prescribed because it does not get absorbed as easily. Our bodies have a hard time breaking ferric iron down into the form that is easiest for us to absorb – ferrous iron. This may be dangerous because an inability to break down iron can lead to iron poisoning. If you are prescribed ferric iron, supplements made with iron citrate are recommended, as this is the easiest form of ferric iron for our bodies to utilize.

What to Look for in Ferrous Iron Supplements

Ferrous iron supplements come in liquid form, capsules, tablets, drops, and extended-release formulas. It is important to look at the "Elemental Iron" amount in an iron supplement before deciding on which is right for you. It is generally agreed that adults with iron deficiency anemia need to receive somewhere between 60 and 200 milligrams of elemental iron.

How to Take Iron Supplements

Whenever embarking upon a new type of medication, there are some guidelines and rules that will apply. Iron supplements are no exception. In order to receive the full benefit of your iron supplement, there are a few rules to follow.

First of all, never take iron supplements with tea, milk, or other dairy products. Unfortunately, calcium has a negative impact on iron absorption and can prevent the desired effects of iron supplementation. It is also important not to combine iron with antacids for similar reasons. You should make sure to time the intake of calcium and antacids so that you do not take them within two hours of taking your iron supplements.

Instead of taking your iron with a glass of milk, it is recommended that you take your iron supplement with orange juice. Orange juice is full of vitamin C, which aids in the absorption of iron in the body. This combination will ensure that as much of the iron supplement makes it into your body as possible.

It is also recommended that iron supplements be taken on an empty stomach. Iron supplements may cause a little bit of stomach upset, so if you really need to, you could take iron supplements with a piece of bread. However, the rule of thumb is to make sure you haven't eaten at least two hours before taking your iron supplement. This ensure that your body is getting as much iron from the supplement as possible. Taking supplements with food can decrease the amount of iron absorbed by up to 60%. This will inevitably result in a longer duration of needing to take iron supplements.

If you are taking your iron supplement in liquid form, make sure that you are mixing it thoroughly in your drink and drinking it with a straw. Unfortunately, iron supplements tend to stain the teeth, even darkening the stool, so it is recommended that a straw is used when taking the supplement. Be sure to brush your teeth thoroughly after drinking a liquid supplement to prevent staining the teeth.

Make sure that you are consuming a lot of liquids when you take your iron supplements. The liquids will help to off-set the common issue of constipation that occurs with iron supplements. Over-the-counter stool softeners are safe to pair with iron supplements if this is an issue for you.

Side Effects of Iron Supplements

As with anything, iron supplements can sometimes be dangerous, particularly if they are taken in doses that are too large for your body to absorb properly. This is why it is so important to have a relationship with a caring and responsible medical practitioner during the duration of treatment for an iron deficiency.

Side effects of iron supplements vary on the inconvenient to the extreme. It is common for stool to look dark, even black, when taking these supplements, but it is dangerous if you notice that stool has blood in it or is tar-like in appearance. Consult your doctor about this immediately and ask about changing your iron supplement if these symptoms occur. You should also mention if you have experienced symptoms such as nausea or stomach upset upon the consumption of iron supplements.

More hazardous issues may occur if you are taking too much iron for your body to handle. For example, you can begin to feel feverish or suffer from headaches, weakened pulse, low blood pressure, chills, and dizziness. Fluid may begin to build up in your lungs and it is even possible to go into a coma if you overdose on iron supplements. This risk is heightened for those who suffer from hemochromatosis, a hereditary condition that causes the body to take in far more iron than it needs. Be careful and always keep your doctor in the loop before making decisions about consumption of iron supplements.

How Long Will It Take for Supplements to Make a Difference?

When we realize that we have a deficiency, it is usually alarming enough that we hope to find an immediate cure. We may even feel impatient to fix the problem right away and feel like the time it takes to heal isn't fast enough.

However, it can take time for the body to begin producing the proper amount of hemoglobin that it needs to produce large, healthy red blood cells that can carry enough oxygen to the body. This is especially true if you have been anemic for a long time without diagnosis or treatment. Patience is the name of the game when it comes to treating anemia.

If the anemia is not too extreme, iron supplements may be able to begin to implement new red cell growth and circulation within a week. Once that begins to happen, upon the initial reception of the iron supplements, hemoglobin should start to rise in a matter of two to three weeks.

Depending on the severity of your anemia, treatment may take as little as eight weeks before the body's red blood cell count and the quality of the hemoglobin are back to normal. However, supplements remain a crucial part of the treatment process for up to two months after the fact, just to make sure the body has enough iron stored for future use. It is important to make sure that the body won't become easily depleted again.

FOODS THAT SUPPORT THE ABSORPTION OF IRON

Oftentimes, an iron deficiency doesn't happen alone. There are many reasons the body might not be receiving enough iron, but if the cause of this complication is dietary, there are other things that need to be taken into consideration before the problem can be fully dealt with.

In order for the body to absorb the proper amount of iron, other nutrients need to be in full supply in the body and able and willing to do their jobs in assisting iron absorption. Without these vitamins and minerals present in the body, there can be complications that may prolong iron deficiency anemia and make it harder for the body to recover.

All of the following nutrients should be taken into consideration when attempting to treat iron deficiency anemia:

- Vitamin C
- Folates
- Vitamin B12

Without the presence of these vitamins and minerals in the body, iron absorption will be difficult, if not impossible.

Vitamin B12 and Iron Absorption

Vitamin B12 and iron have a lot in common. They are both crucial elements when it comes to the production of healthy red blood cells and brain function. Without vitamin B12, the body can suffer both physically and mentally. If long-term depletion of vitamin B12 becomes an issue, it can cause severe anemia and neurological problems.

Vitamin B12 deficiency and iron deficiency are often linked, and symptoms of a vitamin B12 deficiency will be discussed in later chapters involving vegan and vegetarian diets, as this specific issue is most common for people who cut meat out of their diets. Often, vitamin B12 and iron are paired together in animal-based foods, so it is uncommon for people who eat enough meat to have issues with receiving enough vitamin B12.

However, deficiencies may occur if someone suffers from difficulties in their digestive systems. Sometimes it is also hard for the body to absorb liquid forms of vitamin B12. People taking some medications or living with celiac disease, inflammatory bowel disease, pernicious anemia, pancreas disease, or other autoimmune disorders are more prone to suffering from dangerous vitamin B12 deficiencies.

Folates and Iron Absorption

Folates are connected to vitamin B12. They are off-shoots of the B-complex vitamins that are essential in assisting metabolic functions in the body. Without enough folates in the body, iron absorption is limited and, if untreated, can be lethal. Without enough B12 and folates in the body, pernicious anemia may develop. This is much more dangerous than the formation of iron-deficient anemia and involves larger-than-average red blood cells. Deficiencies can usually be easily treated with supplements.

Vitamin C and Iron Absorption

As mentioned previously, vitamin C is usually very helpful in assisting with the treatment of iron-deficient anemia. Most of us don't have a lack of vitamin C, as it is in many common food staples in North America. It is easy to find vitamin C, whether one follows a plant-based diet or a diet rooted in the consumption of animals.

On rare occasions, a vitamin C deficiency may occur, because our bodies do not naturally produce this essential vitamin. Without vitamin C, it is difficult for our bodies to repair themselves, and may lead to unhealthy bones, including teeth and cartilage. The skin is also affected by vitamin C and may become unhealthy without proper amounts of this vitamin in the diet.

The ascorbic acid that is present in vitamin C is essential in enhancing iron absorption. This is especially true in cases of ferrous iron while being less effective in the absorption of ferric acid in the body. It is believed that improper storage and handling of vitamin C products may decrease the efficiency in using ascorbic acid to treat iron deficiency anemia. However, vitamin C remains a critical part in the absorption of iron in the body.

Foods That Assist in the Absorption of Iron

It is clearly very important to maintain a varied diet that is rich in vitamin C, folates, vitamin B12, and iron for the healthy functioning of the body and mind. Because of this, make sure that your body is never lacking in foods rich in these nutrients.

Foods that aid in the absorption of iron in the body include the following:

•Strawberries

•Cherries

•Citrus fruits (oranges, grapefruit, lemons, limes, etc.)

•Papaya

•Kiwi

•Blackcurrant

•Bell peppers

- Guava
- Brussels sprouts
- Melons
- Dark leafy greens
- Broccoli
- Amalaki fruit
- Cauliflower
- Tomatoes
- Cilantro
- Chives
- Thyme
- Basil
- Parsley
- Eggs
- Red meat
- Shellfish
- Fish
- Poultry
- Vitamin B12 fortified foods
- Crab
- Edamame
- Black eyed peas
- Lentils
- Spinach

- Asparagus
- Romaine lettuce
- Avocado
- Mango
- Broccoli
- Wheat bread

All of these foods have levels of either vitamin C, vitamin B12, folates, or combinations of these vitamins that aid the body in absorbing iron. Deficiencies of any of these vitamins can be very dangerous to the system. If you suspect you may have a deficiency, read on through the chapter dedicated to vegans and vegetarians to learn more and consult your doctor.

IRON-RICH FOODS

It may seem obvious by now that eating foods that are rich in iron is a great way to improve the amount of iron consumed in an otherwise low-iron diet. However, this seemingly intuitive knowledge may be difficult for many, particularly those who follow a plant-based diet or lifestyle. While it can be dangerous to lack iron because of dietary preferences, it is still possible to receive adequate amounts of iron if you are persistent and dedicated to meeting your health needs.

Foods that are rich in iron include:

- Organ meats

- Lamb

- Dark meat chicken

- Pork

- Tofu

- Apricots

- Egg yolks

- Legumes

- Beans

- Pumpkin seeds

- Tuna

- Sardines
- Leafy greens
- Spinach
- Collard greens
- Kale
- Oysters
- Shellfish
- Halibut
- Salmon
- Fish
- Red meat
- Raisins
- Poultry
- Chicken
- Turkey
- Whole grains
- Amaranth
- Quinoa
- Iron-fortified breads and cereals
- Prunes
- Dark chocolate
- Potatoes

Without regular consumption of iron-rich foods and the foods that make it possible for our bodies to absorb iron, it can be very difficult for us to live a well-balanced lifestyle. Many issues may arise due to deficiencies, and of any of the things that may complicate iron intake in the body can be dangerous. Because of this, you should always be sure to consult your doctor or nutritionist before adopting a new diet or if you feel that you are at risk of dietary deficiencies. Long-term deficiencies in any of the vitamins or minerals mentioned in this book can lead to serious and sometimes life-long health consequences. It is always better to be thorough and well-informed before taking on a diet that could be potentially dangerous to your health.

LIFESTYLE CHANGES THAT CAN IMPROVE IRON INTAKE

While it can seem daunting to get enough iron in the diet, particularly if you have chosen a diet that is low in iron or you have a difficult time absorbing iron due to other health issues, there are ways that you can begin to supplement iron in your daily life by making a few simple changes.

First, try to consume less coffee, tea, and other caffeinated products. Unfortunately, these products can make it much more difficult for our bodies to absorb iron. While it may seem difficult, especially if you have developed a dependency on caffeine to get you going in the mornings, cutting this component out of your diet can actually help you to feel more energized in the long run and allow your body to absorb more iron.

Improving consumption of foods rich in vitamin B12, folates, and vitamin C is another helpful way to get more iron. If our bodies are having a hard time absorbing iron, whether we are eating enough or not, then health problems are doomed to arise.

Next, it can be important to avoid lead or lead-containing components. If you are working in an environment where you have exposure to lead, this could severely impact your life and make it difficult to avoid anemia. This is particularly true if you are frequently near batteries, paint, or petroleum, or eat with dishes that contain lead in them.

A good way to get more iron in your diet by making a simple lifestyle change is to begin cooking with cast-iron pots and pans. Unfortunately, however, cast iron utensils have been known to contain lead. The lead was used to soften the cast iron for molding. If you are cooking with older cast iron pots and pans, it is more likely that they contain lead substances. You can get these tested to make sure that what you are using to cook with and eat from is actually healthy for the body. Otherwise, you may find yourself at risk of neurological disorders and other conditions.

Another important tip is to look carefully at the ingredients in the foods that you eat. If a food contains the preservative EDTA then it is dangerous to the body and may actually make it more difficult to absorb iron. You should also try to avoid excessive amounts of fiber or calcium in the diet.

It is also useful to try to pair iron-rich foods with foods that assist in the absorption of iron. The recipes section at the end of this book will touch upon a few ideas that can be utilized. Also, instead of eating types of bread that are made of wheat that has been processed and refined into all-purpose white flour, try opting instead for more grainy bread such as those made of barley or other iron-rich whole grains. It may be an adjustment, but it is one that will serve you well and improve your health, with or without iron deficiency anemia.

Last, but not least, if you are able to find a safe cast-iron pot or pan to cook with, cooking foods in these pans and including acidic and vitamin C-rich ingredients, such as lime or lemon juice, will help your food absorb more iron from this cookware. Not only that, but it will also help your body absorb the iron that the food picks up from the pot and help you to consume more iron than you were receiving before, leading to a higher iron intake overall.

What NOT to Eat When Consuming Iron-Rich Foods

We've spoken a bit about what to eat with iron-rich foods to ensure that as much iron is being absorbed by the body as possible, and we've also touched on things to avoid when taking iron supplements that can inhibit iron absorption in the body. Here is a comprehensive list of things to avoid when eating iron-rich foods to ensure that your body is able to absorb as much iron as possible from the foods that you eat. Wait at least two hours before or after eating iron-rich foods to consume the following.

Do NOT consume the following paired with iron-rich foods:

•Caffeinated beverages

•Soda

•Tea

•Coffee

•Antacids

That isn't to say you should never eat these foods if you have iron deficiency anemia. It simply means that you should time the consumption of these things carefully by making sure that you are not eating any of these caffeine or calcium-rich foods during the time your body is attempting to digest and absorb iron. However, it is recommended to cut down caffeine intake overall to ensure greater absorption of iron into the body.

VEGANS, VEGETARIANS, AND IRON DEFICIENCY

One popular reason that many people might suffer from iron deficiency anemia is a plant-based diet. This lifestyle choice may be undertaken with the best of intentions, but without a real knowledge of nutrition and care for the body and its nutritional needs, a vegan and vegetarian diet may leave you lacking the desired nutrients that promote healthy growth and development.

Vegans are especially prone to the limitations that their diets result in, and iron deficiencies coupled with vitamin B12, folate, and calcium deficiencies may all arise as a serious result of irresponsible diet planning. While it is possible to continue on a path of plant-based eating, it can only be done if care and consideration are taken into the consumption of foods that are diverse and rich in vitamins and minerals that support the metabolic system and other important aspects of the body.

Unfortunately, it is a lot less common for vegans and vegetarians born in North America to have proper nutrition, as the diets that ensure healthy results, such as plant-based diets in countries rich in fruits, vegetables, and whole grains, are not as readily available. The Standard American Diet, also known as the SAD diet, does not prepare most people for a healthy execution of the vegan or vegetarian diets, so one must be entirely self-motivated when it comes to seeing to a nutritionally sound way of approaching this lifestyle.

Iron, Folate, and Vitamin B12 Deficiencies in Vegan

and Vegetarian Diets

The sad fact of the matter is that people who live on a plant-based diet for a long time may be neglecting a serious need. Iron, vitamin B12, and folates are generally combined in animal-based foods and consumed together to ensure healthy metabolic systems and blood production. However, once a person decides to embark upon a plant-based diet, that easy source of iron, folates and vitamin B12 are gone.

Without proper nutrition and careful supplementation, nutritional deficiencies can and will occur. The longer you go without diagnosing a nutritional deficiency, the harder it becomes to reverse the results of these dangerous limitations of the body. For example, a vitamin B12 deficiency can permanently reduce brain functioning, harm the memory, and cause lasting damage to the nerves.

These deficiencies are common and often ignored. However, just because we are surviving on the diets that we are on does not mean that our bodies are thriving. And issues later on will crop up, as a result, sometimes even leading to premature death. Take care of your body now rather than suffering later.

How Much Vitamin B12 and Folate Do We Need?

Unless we are deficient in vitamin B12, the amount of this vitamin that we need is surprisingly small. The FDA suggests that we need only consume about 2.4 micrograms of vitamin B12 daily.

What many vegans forget to take into consideration is that the vitamin B12 and folate compound actually work together as part of the B-complex vitamins. Whether or not we consume folic acid won't matter if we aren't receiving enough vitamin B12 to activate it.

It is generally rare to have a vitamin B12 deficiency, but if a plant-based lifestyle is your choice, it is sadly simple. As we age, however, this deficiency can become a lot more common, as our bodies begin to have a hard time absorbing vitamin B12 the older we get. Instead of absorbing the vitamin B12 we receive, we end up eliminating it as a waste product.

As for folates, the recommended daily allowance is as follows:

•Children six months old and younger: 65 micrograms per day

•Children seven months to 12 months of age: 80 micrograms per day

•Children one to three years of age: 150 micrograms per day

•Children four to eight years of age: 200 micrograms per day

•Children nine to 13 years of age: 300 micrograms per day

•Children 14 years of age and older: 400 micrograms per day

•Women who are nursing: 500 micrograms per day

•Women who are pregnant: 600 micrograms per day

If a deficiency is found, your doctor may recommend a higher dosage of a folate supplement. Make sure to follow instructions closely in order to combat folate deficiencies before any long-term harm is done to your body or mind.

Symptoms of Vitamin B12 Deficiency

There are many complications that can arise from a vitamin B12 deficiency. Make sure that you are on top of all of your symptoms and consult a doctor and nutritionist when experiencing symptoms of a vitamin B12 deficiency. Remember, this type of deficiency can make it difficult, if not impossible, to absorb enough iron in the body. Our bodies are made up of systems that work together to function and if one or more areas fail to thrive, that can have a lasting impact on our bodies and minds.

Symptoms of vitamin B12 deficiency include:

•Megaloblastic anemia

•Fatigue

•Pale skin

•Weakness

- Heart palpitations
- Constipation
- Gas
- Vision loss
- Memory loss
- Behavioral changes
- Loss of appetite
- Shortness of breath
- Nerve issues
- Tingling in the arms or legs
- Depression
- Confusion
- Diarrhea
- Shortness of breath

Vitamin B12 deficiency can generally be treated, even if you choose to maintain your vegan or vegetarian lifestyle. If you are not absorbing vitamin B12 as a result of other health problems, that can also generally be treated. For those suffering from health issues outside of their chosen diet, a lifetime of supplements, injections, and nasal therapies meant to help maintain a balance of vitamin B12 can result in a healthier relationship with vitamin B12 for your body.

If you are vegan or vegetarian, a vitamin B12 deficiency is easy to combat and prevent in the future, simply by making conscious dietary choices to include vitamin B12 into your diet. There are supplements, vitamins, and injections that are available to those deficient in vitamin B12 and you should take care to include foods that have been fortified with vitamin B12 so that you do not become deficient in vitamin B12 again.

While these are great ways to work through the symptoms of a vitamin B12 deficiency, there is a sad and lasting problem that cannot always be mended. If the vitamin B12 deficiency was caught too late and caused nerve damage to your body, that is irreversible.

If you suspect you may be suffering from a vitamin B12 deficiency, do everything in your power to get a handle on it and reverse the effects before it is too late. Consult a doctor and be careful when making dietary choices in the future.

HEMOCHROMATOSIS

On the opposite end of the spectrum is an issue known as hemochromatosis. Hemochromatosis is a hereditary condition that makes it difficult to regulate the amount of iron in the body. It usually leads to the over-absorption of iron in the body, which can cause health problems, especially later on in life. Hemochromatosis has several drawbacks and can require a low-iron diet, such as a vegan diet, in order to cope with these symptoms.

What is Hemochromatosis?

Hemochromatosis is the polar opposite of iron deficiency anemia. Instead of making it difficult for the body to absorb iron, it makes it far too easy. Excess iron eventually begins to accumulate within the body, where it is stored in inconvenient locations, such as in the heart, pancreas, or liver. When these organs are burdened by excess stores of iron, it can cause many complications.

Iron is generally absorbed through the intestines and continues to increase the stores of iron in the body that are received through dietary consumption of iron. Unfortunately, because the iron is absorbed rather than expelled through the intestines, it is virtually impossible for people suffering from hemochromatosis to get rid of the excess iron in their bodies.

The body begins to store the iron in the areas mentioned above, with areas such as the adrenal glands, gonads, and joints also being affected. Complications include cirrhosis, lack of adrenaline, diabetes, heart failure, and poly-arthropathy.

When you are diagnosed with hemochromatosis, you are not likely to be given iron supplements of any kind, as this can result in a toxic overload that would prove fatal to a person suffering from this disorder.

Symptoms of Hemochromatosis

Hemochromatosis can be difficult to pinpoint until later on in life when symptoms become more severe. Early warning signs were mentioned previously in the book, but we will mention them here again, with a few more included.

Warning signs and symptoms of hemochromatosis include:

- Fatigue
- Incontinence
- Joint pain
- Bone pain
- Insulin resistance
- Congestive heart failure
- Malaise
- Lethargy
- Adrenal gland damage
- Lack of adrenaline
- Abnormal heart rhythms
- Erectile dysfunction
- Liver cirrhosis or jaundice
- Decreased libido

- Hypogonadism
  - Arthritis, particularly in the knee, shoulder, and the second and third MCP joints in the hands
- Organ damage

Less frequently, symptoms and complications may also include:

- Susceptibility to disease
- Deafness
- Pituitary and parathyroid gland dysfunction
- Dark or gray colored pigmentation of the skin
- Hair loss
- Hypothyroidism
- Osteoporosis

Overall, while the symptoms of hemochromatosis may be difficult to catch early on, the more damage this disease does over time, the more dangerous it can become.

Treating Hemochromatosis

Hemochromatosis, while a complex genetic disease, is also one that can be lived with, using specific methods of keeping this disorder in check. If caught early, you have a much higher chance of preventing some of the more dangerous side effects of toxic iron buildup in the body and organs.

Treatments such as the application of desferrioxamine mesylate and bloodletting can be utilized in order to help remove excessive iron stores to the blood. You may also be instructed to change your diet to one that is less rich in iron and the components that aid in the absorption of iron.

For example, you will want to limit foods listed previously that are rich in vitamin C, and avoid alcohol, red meat, and seafood. The foods that limit iron absorption should be utilized, such as black and tannin-rich teas and calcium.

It can seem bleak to live with hemochromatosis. However, just do your best and listen to your doctors. While there can be some complications, it is possible to live a comfortable life with this condition, especially when it is caught early on.

LOW-IRON RECIPE IDEAS FOR SUFFERERS OF HEMOCHROMATOSIS

People who suffer from hemochromatosis may find that their options seem somewhat limited when they are reduced to trying to live on a low-iron diet. Most people are used to being able to eat meat whenever they want to, and the complications that can arise from hemochromatosis can be varied and significant, depending upon the specific conditions your body is facing.

The recipes and ideas in this chapter are not going to be useful for everybody. Many people with hemochromatosis also suffer from diseases that already have specific dietary restrictions, such as type 2 diabetes. Please use common sense and consult your doctor or nutritionist before implementing any of these ideas into your lifestyle.

It isn't so bad to eat a low-iron diet once you get the hang of it, so hopefully, with these ideas and tips in mind, you will find it somewhat easier to cope with hemochromatosis and still enjoy foods that you thought you would miss when you were diagnosed with hemochromatosis.

Breakfast Recipe: Homemade Low-Iron Cereal

Serving Size: 1

Prep Time: 6 minutes

Cook Time: N/A

Ingredients

- 1 cup shredded wheat, Trader Joe brand
- 1 tsp. cinnamon
- 1 tsp. stevia
- 1 banana
- ¼ cup rhubarb
- 1 tsp. already brewed black tea
- Whole milk

Instructions

1. Mix all dry ingredients together in a medium-sized bowl.
2. Pour in whole milk (use your own discretion here) and add 1 tsp. of black tea.
3. Mix thoroughly and enjoy!

Lunch Recipe: Low-Iron Chicken Soup

Serving Size: 4

Prep Time: 20 minutes

Cook Time: 30 minutes

Ingredients

- 1 lb. pure white chicken breast
- 2 carrots
- 1 onion
- 3 tomatoes
- 1 stick celery
- ½ cup sour cream
- 1 cup water
- 2 boiled eggs
- ½ cup already brewed black tea
- 1 cup shredded cheddar cheese

Instructions

1. Bring a cup of water and a half cup of black tea to a boil.

2. In the meantime, shred chicken and chop vegetables.

3. Place chicken in the broth once boiling and allow to cook for 15 minutes.

4. After 15 minutes, add in the vegetables, boiled eggs, and half of your sour cream.

5. Allow to cook for another 15 minutes. Serve hot and top with sour cream and shredded cheese.

Dinner Recipe: Low-Iron Turkey Chili

Serving Size: 3

Prep Time: 20 minutes

Cook Time: 45 minutes

Ingredients

- 8 oz. ground turkey
- 6 oz. can of kidney beans
- ¼ cup diced onions
- ½ cup already brewed black tea
- 6 oz. diced tomatoes
- 3 oz. tomato paste
- ½ tsp. red pepper flakes
- 2 tsp. olive oil
- Salt and pepper to taste

Instructions

1. Heat a saucepan over medium heat. Pour in the oil and allow to get hot.
2. Once hot, fry the onion until golden brown and translucent.
3. Add the meat and cook with the onions until brown.
4. Pour in diced tomatoes and tomato paste. Mix and allow the combination to simmer for about 10 minutes.
5. Add in the brewed black tea, spices, and kidney beans.
6. Allow to come to a boil before covering and turning the heat on low.
7. Simmer together for half an hour and then serve hot.

Snack Recipe: Matcha Smoothie

Serving Size: 2

Prep Time: 5 minutes

Cook Time: 3 minutes

Ingredients

- 1 banana
- ½ cup frozen raspberries
- ½ cup frozen blueberries
- 1 cup already brewed matcha tea
- 1 tbsp. already brewed black tea
- 5 ice cubes

Instructions

1. Place all ingredients into a high-speed blender.
2. Blend on high until smooth.
3. Serve immediately.

Tips

Unfortunately, it is not good for people with hemochromatosis to eat red meat that is full of iron, or starchy pasta and breads that are made with grains containing iron, so it can seem like options are limited. However, there may be some recipes available that accommodate your specific dietary restrictions if you look into raw vegan cooking.

Another option for hemochromatosis sufferers is to look into vegan cookbooks and consult your doctor. There are often cookbooks readily available for those who are diagnosed with hemochromatosis, so don't be afraid to ask. It can be a difficult diet to get accustomed to.

Last but not least, because hemochromatosis is a genetic condition, make sure that you are adamant about getting your children and other family members tested if it turns out that you are suffering from hemochromatosis. Even though it is not detected until later in life, that is only because of the complications this condition can cause. Be responsible and share your knowledge of this condition with your friends and family members. Remember, knowledge is power!

IRON-RICH RECIPES FOR VEGANS AND VEGETARIANS

Eating a plant-based diet can be hard enough without having to worry about deficiencies everywhere you look. Unfortunately, the fact of the matter remains that you will probably have to be willing to take iron and vitamin B12 supplements if you pursue a plant-based diet.

That being said, it is still possible to enjoy living life to the fullest and enjoying the foods that you eat. Making sure that you eat nutrient-rich foods that help you to prevent the depletion of vitamins and minerals in your body can help to ensure that no matter what you are eating, you are full of vital life energy and ready to take on the world.

Deficiencies in iron and vitamin B12 can leave the brain feeling murky and cloudy, but utilizing the following recipes and tips will allow you to continue living a vegan or vegetarian lifestyle without having to compromise your ethical values for your health and nutrition needs.

Breakfast Recipe: Cinnamon Sugar Quinoa with Raisins

Serving Size: 2

Prep Time: 10 minutes

Cook Time: 10 minutes

Ingredients

- 1 cup quinoa
- 2 cups water
- ¼ cup agave nectar
- 1 tbsp. cinnamon
- 1 tbsp. raisins
- 1 tbsp. roasted almonds

Instructions

1. Bring water to a boil.
2. Add quinoa and stir until all water is absorbed.
3. Stir in cinnamon and raisins.
4. Pour into a serving bowl and top with agave nectar and roasted almonds.
5. Serve immediately.

Lunch Recipe: Iron-Rich Edamame Salad

Serving Size: 2

Prep Time: 10 minutes

Cook Time: N/A

Ingredients

- 1 cup edamame
- 1 cup spinach
- 1 cup kale
- 1 mandarin orange, peeled and separated into pieces
- ½ cup walnuts
- ¼ cup shredded carrot

Instructions

1. Combine all ingredients together in a large salad bowl.
2. Top with shredded carrots and walnuts.
3. Serve immediately.

Dinner Recipe: Iron-Rich Vegetarian Chili

Servings: 6

Prep Time: 12 hrs. 15 minutes

Cook Time: 30 minutes

Ingredients

- 4 oz. lentils
- 4 oz. kidney beans
- 3 oz. black-eyed peas
- 2 cups textured vegetable protein
- 2 cups water
- 1 carrot
- 5 tomatoes
- 1 zucchini
- 1 onion
- 1 tsp. red pepper flakes
- 1 tsp. cumin
- 1 tsp. sweet chili powder

Instructions

1. Soak the beans and lentils for 12 hours or overnight to make it easier for the body to digest them.

2. Chop up the onion, zucchini, tomatoes, and carrot.

3. Add all ingredients into a slow cooker (or boil them together over medium heat for approximately four hours and 30 minutes).

4. Allow cooking in the slow cooker on high heat for two hours.

5. Serve immediately.

Snack Recipe: Vegan Kale Chips

Serving Size: 6

Prep Time: 10 minutes

Cook Time: 15 minutes

Ingredients

- 1 batch of organic kale
- 1 tbsp. extra virgin coconut oil
- 1 tbsp. nutritional yeast flakes
- 1 tsp. salt

Instructions

1. Preheat your oven to 350 degrees Fahrenheit.

2. Chop up your kale into bite-sized pieces. Wash it well and dry before baking.

3. Place kale on a cookie sheet lined with parchment paper. Pour melted coconut oil over the kale and then sprinkle with nutritional yeast flakes and salt.

4. Bake for 15 minutes, until edges are crisp and brown.

5. Serve immediately.

Tips

If you are living with an iron deficiency, which is very common on a vegan or vegetarian diet, or if you are simply hoping to prevent iron deficiency anemia from happening in your life as a result of your lifestyle, it is important that you are able to eat the right types of foods.

As mentioned previously, do not pair iron-rich foods with foods that can inhibit the absorption of iron into your body. This can be very dangerous for you, particularly when you are already having a hard enough time in getting the iron that you need from your diet. A good way to make sure you are getting enough iron from these foods is to make sure that you are separating the time you eat these iron-rich foods from the times you are eating foods full of calcium. Make sure these chunks of time are separated by at least two hours before and after eating iron for the maximum impact of iron absorption.

For the best results, make sure that you are eating in a smart way. Use foods in good combinations, such as eating iron-rich foods paired with foods that are full of vitamin C. Here is a list of foods that make good pairs with iron-rich foods, such as lentils, leafy greens, and beans.

- Tomatoes
- Squash
- Broccoli
- Citrus
- Foods rich in vitamin B12
- Foods rich in folate

If you eat responsibly, then you will be able to avoid issues with iron absorption in your body. Whether you have already proven deficient in iron or vitamin B12 and folates, or you are simply hoping to avoid the worst-case scenario from happening, there are still great options for vegans and vegetarians to enjoy their diets and still hold firmly to their moral standing.

Although it can be dangerous to live a lifestyle that makes it difficult to receive adequate nutrition, there are many supplements out there that can help you to make the choice to be vegan or vegetarian responsibly, without suffering from the adverse health effects, such as iron deficiency. However, you have to be adamant about holding true to the dietary needs and demands that your body will make on you. Otherwise, you will have nobody to blame but yourself for the consequences of living your life in an unhealthy way.

Many might think it is a stupid choice to live a vegan or vegetarian lifestyle because of the health risks it may pose, but there is no reason to hesitate if you are willing to look past these dangers and walk the extra mile to ensure that you are as healthy as possible.

IRON-RICH RECIPES AND TIPS FOR MEAT-EATERS

Possibly the most common type of diet that people in North America follow to is a meat-based diet. Fortunately, most red meats are high in iron, B12, and folate, so eating red meat is a great way to help to combat iron deficiency anemia. While it can still be problematic when anemia is caused by other extenuating circumstances, there are several great recipes and food combinations that can be utilized by people who are hoping to prevent and combat iron deficiency anemia.

Breakfast Recipe: Iron-Rich Spinach and Bacon Omelet

Serving Size: 2

Prep Time: 5 minutes

Cook Time: 10 minutes

Ingredients

- 5 large eggs
- 1 cup spinach
- 1 tomato
- 3 strips bacon

- 1 tbsp. olive oil

Instructions

1. Preheat the oil in a skillet over medium heat.

2. Beat eggs and wash and shred spinach, and wash and dice tomato.

3. Once the oil is hot, fry bacon until crispy and remove from heat.

4. Mix spinach and tomato into the egg batter and then pour into the skillet.

5. Allow cooking until firm on the bottom, about four minutes.

6. As it cooks, dice the fried bacon.

7. Flip the omelet over and allow to fry until a coating develops.

8. Place the bacon in the middle of the omelet and then fold the omelet in half.

9. Allow to fry on both sides evenly until golden brown.

10. Serve immediately.

Lunch Recipe: Iron-Rich Potato and Beef Stew

Serving Size: 6 servings

Prep Time: 20 minutes

Cook Time: 30 minutes

Ingredients

- 1 lb. beef
- 5 potatoes
- 5 carrots
- 12 oz. lentils
- 1 onion

- 1 tbsp. olive oil
- 6 cups water

Instructions

1. In a skillet, heat a tablespoon of olive oil.
2. Dice onions.
3. Fry the onions until golden brown and translucent.
4. Fry the beef until browned.
5. Once finished, peel potatoes and wash thoroughly. Dice them into bite-sized pieces and set aside.
6. Fill a soup pot with six cups of water.
7. Pour in all ingredients, including the oil from cooking the beef and onions.
8. Cover the pot and bring the water to a boil.
9. Once boiling, reduce to a simmer and allow to cook for about 20 minutes.
10. Remove from heat and then serve hot.

Dinner Recipe: Iron-Rich Steak and Potato Dinner

Serving Size: 2 servings

Prep Time: 1 hour and 15 minutes

Cook Time: 20 minutes

Ingredients

- 1 16 oz. steak
- 3 cloves of garlic
- 1 cup of soy sauce
- 2 potatoes

- 1 head of broccoli
- 1 tbsp. olive oil
- 1 tsp. butter
- Salt and pepper to taste

Instructions

1. In a large container, pour soy sauce.

2. Peel and mince garlic.

3. Place the steak in the soy sauce and pour the garlic into the container. Allow marinating for an hour (longer if you prefer).

4. When the steak is sufficiently marinated, wash potatoes and cut large slices in the center of them. Bake for 40 minutes.

5. In a large skillet, heat the olive oil over medium-high heat.

6. Fry the steak over medium heat. Flip when golden brown on the bottom and allow to cook all the way through until steak reaches the desired consistency.

7. Remove from heat and set aside. Use the steak grease to fry the broccoli until bright green or to your preferred texture.

8. Once potatoes are finished, top with butter and serve immediately.

Dessert Recipe: Iron-Rich Roasted Pumpkin Seeds

Serving Size: 2 servings

Prep Time: 10 minutes

Cook Time: 45 minutes

Ingredients

- 2 cups raw pumpkin seeds
- 2 ½ tsp. melted butter

- 1 tsp. cinnamon
- 1 tsp. nutmeg
- 1 tsp. brown sugar

Instructions

1. Preheat oven to 300 degrees Fahrenheit.

In a large mixing bowl, combine all ingredients together.

2. Stir until thoroughly combined.

3. Pour the pumpkin seeds onto a baking sheet that is lined with parchment paper.

4. Bake the pumpkin seeds at the same temperature for approximately 45 minutes, or until golden brown. Make sure that you stir them every 13 minutes.

5. Serve warm and store in a cool dry container.

Tips

Fortunately for people who live on a meat-based diet, it is easier than it would be for someone who is vegan or vegetarian to receive an adequate amount of iron, B12, folate, and calcium. It can still be challenging if low iron is a result of other health issues.

All of the recipes above are great when partnered with ingredients that are rich in vitamin B12 and folate. Try not to eat foods rich in calcium too soon before or after eating the iron rich foods above. This is the best way to guarantee that iron is readily absorbed into the body using the foods that are introduced through these recipes.

You can also look through several cookbooks, keeping the helpful iron-rich ingredients in mind and supplement ingredients that other people use with those that you know are high in iron content. That way, you will be able to enjoy readily-available iron-rich food sources that are close to the foods that you already know and love. It is a good way to help you get a little bit more creative in the kitchen so that you don't have to try too hard to think about all of the different ways you can use food to help you to supplement iron in your diet.

Try to always cook your meats and vegetables with cast iron skillets and pots so that your food absorbs extra iron from the cookware. It is a great way to enrich foods that are low in iron and give them a boost. Some places sell blocks of iron that you can add to your soup pots or pans that allow iron to leach into your foods. These blocks are available in different designs and are another interesting way to incorporate more iron into your diet.

No matter what you choose to do, try not to get discouraged if you are suffering from an iron deficiency and instead address it responsibly. It can be difficult to re-train yourself to think about iron as an important part of your diet, but if you are able to eat meat and you understand the ins and outs of iron absorption in the body, you are well on your way to great health!

10 STEPS AHEAD

Trying to incorporate a low iron diet into your life can be a challenge, just as it can be challenging to live with an iron deficiency. There are many ins and outs to iron absorption in the body, and unfortunately, if you are having an issue absorbing iron, there could be many causes and many other complications associated with this.

Iron deficiency is one of the leading vitamin deficiencies in North America and we are fortunate that there has been so much research done to help us understand just what it means to be iron deficient. When we are coping with any type of deficiency in the body, it can lead to a multitude of problems. Our bodies are very efficient systems and when one thing goes wrong, it can often be the beginning of many other types of problems.

Thankfully, it is relatively simple to treat and prevent an iron deficiency if the primary cause of the deficiency is diet-based. Other types of anemia can be more complex, but they are also easily dealt with through supplements and other dietary changes. People who find out that they are not absorbing enough iron, or who are absorbing too much iron, may have to undergo some difficult lifestyle changes, but despite a difficulty in adapting, it can be a very beneficial transition to make.

Whether you are a vegan or vegetarian whose diet simply lacks iron, vitamin B12, and folates, or you are suffering from anemia for another reason, iron deficiency is a common issue that usually doesn't cause lasting damage. Left untreated, however, anemia and other vitamin deficiencies related to anemia can become very dangerous.

Consulting with your doctor is an important step in the process of dealing with iron deficiencies or iron overload in the body. With the help of a qualified medical professional, you will be able to understand the inadequacies in your diet and deal with them in a more in-depth way that is guaranteed to help you feel better as soon as possible.

It is important that you educate yourself as well, and hopefully, after reading this book, you will feel more prepared to tackle whatever lies ahead in the future, whether you are trying to cope with an iron deficiency, iron overload, or you simply want to prevent the worst case scenario from happening to you.

It is possible to live your life in a healthy and rewarding way, even if you find yourself facing health problems. The trick is to always stay positive and remain mindful of the choices that you make and how they might affect your body. Try to think 10 steps ahead when it comes to your health. And even if it feels like it's too late, don't buy into that negative mindset. There is always time to make positive changes and better yourself, for yourself.

No matter where you fall with your health, knowledge is power and you do have the power to be as healthy as you can possibly be. Make the choices that are best for your lifestyle and always be prepared to look into the future, at least 10 steps ahead. No matter what the future might bring, you can prepare yourself and take comfort in the fact that you are doing your best to be the best version of yourself that you can possibly be. If you are on your own team, everything will turn out fine.

Printed in Great Britain
by Amazon